Jimmy Buffett's Hawaii

Twenty four original watercolors
reproduced for framing

Published by

Cameron and Company

San Francisco, California

Cameran and Company
235 Montgomery Street
San Francisco, California 94104

First Printing 1980
Second Printing 1983

Library of Congress Catalog Number: 80.67292
Guy Buffet's Hawaii ISBN 0-918684-11-0.

I acknowledge to the following my thanks and Aloha
for their friendship and assistance:
Gwen Akana and Henk Kuiper, Charles Feeney, James Killett,
Mr & Mrs Gabby Pahinui and all Hawaiian musicians,
"Chavi" Lou Campbell and Rev Charley Burger, Mr Alfred Preis,
Mr & Mrs Carl Lindquist, Mr & Mrs Peter Radulovic, Michel,
Mr & Mrs Chuck Mc Crary, Jane and Richard Peltz, Donald Onush,
Colonel Alex Wilson, "Mémé" Laura Belisle and Nicole Timon Buffet
Sue and Rory Calhoun, Lahaina Gallery and Kapalua Gallery. Maui. Hawaii

For Special editorial assistance I am grateful to Ronn Ronck

Book design by Jane Olang Kristiansen
Printed in Japan

For my wife Joanie

Me Ke Aloha

Captain James Cook arrives in Hawaii

Captain James Cook arrives in Hawaii

Captain Cook, the greatest sailor of his time, sighted the Hawaiian Islands in 1778. This painting commemorating that event, was done in 1971. It marks the beginning of my current "whimsical" style.

That painting created enough interest for the Honolulu Magazine to run a four pages story about it. under the title "a most irreverent Frenchman". Although unintentional I was the first one to treat that most important event in such a manner. It didn't create the controversy that some people had feared and it turned out to be the most popular painting that I had during a show at the Mauna Kea Beach Hotel where it was bought by the Reverend & Mrs Alex Campbell of Maui.

1980 Arrival of a Japanese group at Honolulu airport.

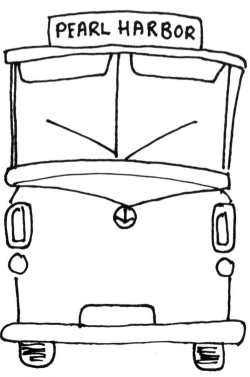

Landing of La Perouse on Maui

Landing of La Perouse on Maui.

While Captain James Cook was the first European to see Maui, he did not attempt to land - that honor went to a Frenchman, Admiral Jean François Galaup, Count De La Perouse. This was in 1786, land was still cheap then and condominiums completely unknown. I am quite certain that La Perouse gave the Mauians a taste the "Joie de Vivre" and this is the theme of that painting.

Portuguese came later on and brought a lot of joy and a lot of jokes to this island and a lot of people are there today not really knowing where they are.

Hey! Captain Medeiros dondn't you think it's awfully hot for Alaska?

Hey Man! Where am I?

PUNA BUTTER

Even today some people do not know where they are ...and probably never will.

Arrival of La Pérouse
on Maui

BORDEA' PINOT BLAN'

CHAMPAGNE

Hawaii: Early days

Hawaii: Early days.

Here we have a group of 19th century Hawaiians, who have come out of their houses and are posing in front of their town. I like to think that they are posing for a painter in much the same manner that people today would pose for a photographer. The style I've used is that of primitive folk artists. It is different from the others in this book but it is not an experiment.

Although that style proves to be very successful among gallery audiences I don't intend to become an Hawaiian Grandma Moses.

1st PRICE
Academy of Arts

Waikiki

Waikiki

Although I first came to Hawaii in 1963, I didn't get around to painting Waikiki and Diamond Head until 1979. It was a subject I avoided because everybody else did it, and to put it frankly I didn't see that much beauty about it. When my publisher asked me to do Waikiki beach for the cover of a calendar, I turned my mental block into a challenge.

I found out that the best way to approach the subject is with a certain sense of humor. Then just by looking around one can find plenty to do . . . . .

DON HO SHOW

SOLD OUT

DUTY FREE

Carnation Fields

Carnation Fields

There is no question in my mind that if Vincent Van Gogh had come to the Hawaiian Islands he would have turned our carnation fields into one of his masterpieces. Looking at them in the midday sun, like a living sea of colors under the trade winds is mind blowing. Hawaii's fantastic light brings all this to my eyes in a great exploding rainbow.

the Quiltmakers

The Quiltmakers.

Sewing was the first western handicraft taught to the Hawaiians by the Calvinist-Christian missionaries when they arrived here in 1820. The native appliqued quilts, with patterns based loosly on plant and animal form, became an indigenous folk art.

In this painting the quilt is the center of attention but to me the women are just as important. I enjoyed blending the fabric of the quilt into the material of their dresses.

This is really a play on shapes and colors. As the women became part of the quilt, the quilt became part of the women.

Riders near a Waterfall

Riders near a waterfall.

This is a kind of imaginary Hawaiian landscape that I do quite often. All of them are done in my studio. The Hawaiian scenery is so spectacular, that one's imagination goes wild and leads to any kind of creativity. When I lived on the big island of Hawaii I did go horseback riding a lot, sometimes with friends for an entire day through misty forests and little known trails. Such rides were so beautiful that we wished they'd never end.

Hawaiian Paniolo.

Maui Riding through Haleakala National Park

talk story

Talk Story.

Here is a good example of how my Hawaiian and tahitian paintings blend into each other.
It could represent either place. Actually I could call it "Hawaiians visiting their tahitian
friends". All over the Pacific there is a certain life style that is shared by all, the
people gather like this in outdoor shelters to gossip, sing song and drink.
Everytime I look at this painting I want to step into it. and say.
"Hey! howzit you guys!"

Samoans at Honolulu Airport waiting for their flight to Pago Pago.

Surfer Watching Waves

Surfer watching waves.

All my art, with few exceptions, has a tendancy towards disproportion. I play around with reality, changing either the people or the landscape.

The surf in this painting, for example, almost becomes a tidal wave. It wasn't really that big when I saw it. The house and trees weren't that close to the beach either.

I use my brushes just as a photographer might use various lenses to create his own vision. This painting was done before my Waimanalo Library mural and was later incorporated into it.

Sunday Morning Before Church

Sunday Morning Before Church.

The first thing one realizes in this painting is that the chair is out of proportion with the rest of the picture. The little girl will have to jump off to reach the floor. When people ask me why I made such a big chair I don't have a definite answer. It is possible that the child represents my own childhood when everything seemed so big to me. Only the girl and her dog are looking at the viewer. Her father reads the Sunday paper and her mother is busy putting on lipstick. I enjoy going to church in Hawaii because everybody dresses in their brightest colors.

Lahaina: Waterfront and Court House

Lahaina: Waterfront and Courthouse

Once the playground of Hawaii's Kings and Queens, Lahaina means "cruel" or "unmerciful sun." This old whaling port on Maui barely averages one foot of rain a year. Lahaina has a number of historic buildings. It's picturesque Courthouse is to Lahaina what the Sacre Coeur is to Paris. Nearly every artist who visits here has painted it, I chose to do it a little bit differently, changing the angle somewhat and making the west Maui mountains higher than they really are. The only way you can see the Courthouse like this is from a boat.

Hasegawa General Store

Hasegawa General Store

Located in Hana, Hasegawa General Store is one of Hawaii's most famous country stores. It's been celebrated in films, books and songs! Outside the Store I've painted a mingling of both local people and tourists. Inside the store has everything you can think of. Once I found a set of my Maui prints hanging from clothespins on a strand of barbed wire.

The dogs in Hana are quite noticeable for their bodies are covered with scars, and have ears and tails missing here and there. That because most of them are wild pig hunters. Very well known among them is "Rusty" whose place on a back of a pick up truck is right above the wheel, therefore everybody recognizes "Rusty" with his half shaved tail.

Hana, Hasegawa's General Store

tiny counting his ducks

Tiny counting his ducks.

People tell me stories and that's how I get much of my inspiration for paintings. When I visited Hana, on Maui, I heard all sorts of tales about Tiny, a true Hawaiian with a heart full of Aloha.

But Tiny is not tiny. He weighs about 300 pounds and has a "ranch" near the ocean. Each night after he comes home, Tiny sits outside with a case of beer and starts counting his ducks. He wants to make sure they've all here, that none is missing or stolen. By the time he finishes the last beer, he has to count them all over again.

CAUTION
BABY PIGS
CROSSING

Road to Hana.

Harry Maui, tiny, counting his ducks

Gatsby

Gabby

I seldom do portraits but I couldn't resist painting Gabby Pahinui, one of Hawaii's best-known local musicians. This painting was started at his house in Waimanalo but I put him near the ocean because I wanted to show him outdoors.

On the rocks are little girls or Hawaiian Menehunes in the nude. I am not sure why I painted them in the picture instead of some animals.

Since one of Gabby's familiar songs is "Sunshine Ladies", maybe we both share the same type of fantasy. I often dream of finding a paradise full of these little creatures.

Gabby's music has had a tremendous influence upon my work. When I listen to it I always get some warm feelings into my soul.

Maui: going night fishing

Maui, Going night fishing

Everything I've read about tropical nights is true and better,
the soft trade winds caressing your body.
the fragrance of the sleeping forest.
the sound of the waves breaking on the distant reef.
the sight of a million stars

Maui Going night fishing

Dog smelling a flower

Dog smelling a flower.

This little dog could be me. I would be smiling too if I had two beautiful girls giving me so much attention. In most Hawaiian legends the animals are given human characteristics, they think and do things like people. Dogs seem to appear in my paintings more than any other animals. It is perhaps that I do share with them this love for freedom. This desire to roam all day long on sunny beaches....

The two women are probably sisters, out gathering fresh flowers to make leis for their friends, or maybe..... for me

Aloha. Ilio O. Palani.

Cans on Roller Skates

Cows on Roller Skates.

My little girl Nicole is a great source of inspiration to me. I tell her stories and she tells me stories. We both thought of cows wearing sneackers and drinking Pepsi light, of monsters running thru the night in pink pantyhoses, of dragons giving up smoking to improve their singing. All kids are wonderful, with their world full of magic and dreams. To put their ideas on canvas is not a joke or a put.on but a pure expression of joy.

Cows on Roller Skates is one of those expressions and they"ll be more to come, as life without fantasy and humor would be pretty dull.

The real joke can be found in some Museums, Galleries and art reviews where things are; minimal, visceral, cosmic, comic and....... boring.

three birds

Three birds,

Birds are a different kind of pet. You cannot pick them up and give a big squeeze. My birds are merely observers.

In this painting they will not stay around too long. If they frightened they will just lift their wings and fly away.

Birds take a good part in the Hawaiian Legends they are mostly friendly "aumakua" which are personal and Gods.

In this painting those three birds could be Loved Ones long time gone from this found lady's life.

Haleiwa

Haleiwa

This country town, a surfing community on the North Shore of Oahu, has a lot of charm. What's disturbing to the eyes, however, and what I emphasize in this painting, is the commercialization of Haleiwa.

When I drive down the main street, my senses are bombarded with images. These stayed in my mind as I began this painting.

The style is abstract. It started as a loose line drawing before I turned it into a watercolor.

Hawaiian Love Song

Hawaiian Love Song

This is a painting that ended up in Waimanalo as part of a mural I did for the Library. It is an interesting mixture of reality with a little myth thrown in. Besides the musician and his sleeping lady friend, you can see a few of the animal characters that appeared in some of the Hawaiian legend books I did. The inspiration for this painting, however, came from music and not from words. I wanted to capture the song of the guitarist, the ocean, the wind, the birds and everything else in the picture.

This is a visual poem and Love Song for Joan, my wife and best friend.

Tita and Friends

Tita and friends.

Tita means sister. This painting is of a young lady going back to the beautiful country where as a little girl she learned to love and respect all living things

This scene is very whimsical, it's a dream in which all her friends came to pay a visit and share with her their Love and Aloha.

Iam feeling blue

Caw feeling blue

If I had an advice to give to young artists, I would tell them not to be afraid to put down on paper whatever comes to their minds, as if they have true feelings nothing will ever be ridiculous. I started doing this painting with one caw, then I painted her blue, because that's the way I saw her in my mind, the following came by itself. A certain feeling and relationship started to develop between those three caws, something happened that affected each one on a different level. Lots of my paintings tell a story, a fable and it's up to each individual to get the moral from each of them.

From "Secret of Beaver Valley"

xii. Cow feeling blue

Olomana Wahine

Olomana Wāhine

Sooner or later, every artist who paints in Hawaii, attempts to portray the legendary Polynesian woman. This is also a favorite subject with the general public. Most of us Frenchmen are fond of three things, beautiful women, good wine and tasty food, not necessarily in that order, but nevertheless all of them important. Being a faithful husband it is safer for me to portray myself as this little dog, having an intimate relationship with this lovely lady.

I told you, just the wine and the food!

The Road to Hana: Little frogs playing by a waterfall

The Road to Hana: Little frogs playing by a waterfall.

It started as a joke. My dearest friend Alex Wilson is a retired Colonel of the Marine Corps. is about 6"2 and I am 5"7. We've been playing tennis for the longest time and on the courts we stand like a Jeff and Mutt. team. this is during one of those game that Alex started calling me "Zee little Frog" I wasn't offended and from that day on I start calling him "La Grande Turkey". True friendships are very hard to come by. and when it does happen one should look at it as a wonderful blessing. This is this kind of a great friendship we have.
I did quite a few paintings related to frogs such as "Frog convention in Waikiki" "Frogs in a discotheque" "the Miss America frog beauty contest. and they've been very popular especially among turkeys.

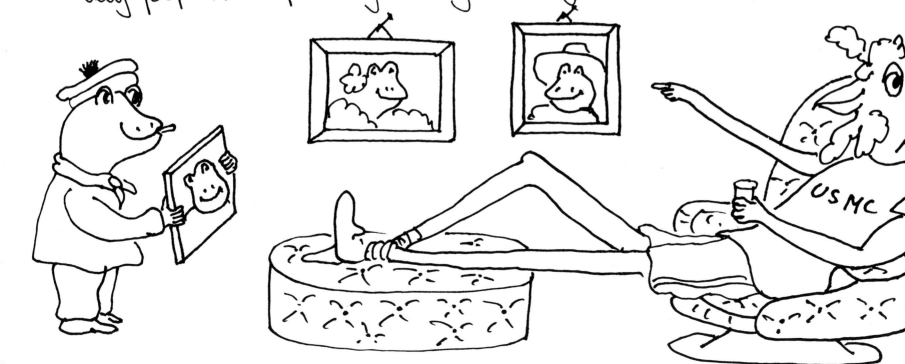

road to Hana: little frogs resting by a waterfall